HAL LEONARD KEYBOARD STYLE SERIES

NEW AGE PIANO

THE COMPLETE GUIDE W

BY TODD LOWRY

ISBN 978-1-4803-3160-0

HAL•LEONARD®
CORPORATION

7777 W. BLUEMOUND RD. P.O. BOX 13819 MILWAUKEE, WI 53213

In Australia contact:
Hal Leonard Australia Pty. Ltd.
4 Lentara Court
Cheltenham, Victoria, 3192 Australia
Email: ausadmin@halleonard.com.au

INTRODUCTION

Welcome to *New Age Piano*. If you've always wanted to play new age piano in the style of George Winston, David Lanz, Jim Brickman, and others, then you've come to the right place. Whatever your playing level, this book will help you develop your new age piano style.

We'll define "new age piano" and trace its history as a musical movement. Then we'll dig into the musical techniques that are vital to the new age pianist.

George Winston suggests on his website that the most important thing for the musician is learning chords. We'll take his advice and begin with chord theory – chord types, inversions, voicings, and progressions. Then we'll discuss left-hand accompaniment styles. We'll examine melodic ideas, motivic development, and musical form. Then we'll suggest ways to put all the elements together to make your own new age piano music.

For each musical technique, we'll include examples for you to practice. By practicing these examples, you can develop the facility to utilize the musical elements in your own playing.

In the last section, the "Style File," you'll find six complete new age compositions in the styles of various new age pianists, incorporating the skills and techniques studied in the book.

You can find many printed folios of new age piano transcriptions in your local music store or at www.halleonard.com. These allow pianists who read music to play the new age style. But the soul of new age piano music consists in developing your own personal style. This book is the place to begin.

Good luck with your New Age Piano!

–Todd Lowry

About the CD

On the accompanying CD, you'll find demonstrations of most of the musical examples in the book. All the tracks feature solo piano. The left-hand part is on the left channel and the right-hand part is on the right channel, for easy "hands separate" practice. A metronome beat accompanies each track. For tracks in 4/4 time, there are four beats before the music begins. For tracks in 3/4, 6/8, or 9/8 time, there are six beats before the music begins.

About the Author

Todd Lowry has written several keyboard instructional books for Hal Leonard Corporation, including *Best of Blues Piano*, *Today's Piano Greats*, and *New Orleans Piano Styles*. A former staff arranger for Hal Leonard, he created hundreds of music folios, including *The Complete Beatles*. In his varied career, Todd has been music supervisor at a major theme park, music critic for a major daily newspaper, and a working jazz pianist. His arrangements appeared on a Grammy-nominated album. He lives in Albuquerque, New Mexico.

Websites of Interest

www.newagemusic.com
www.newagemusicworld.com
www.newagepiano.net
www.solopianoradio.com

CONTENTS

Chapter 1

WHAT IS NEW AGE PIANO?

New age music is an umbrella term for a variety of musical styles intended to create relaxation, artistic inspiration, and optimism.

Pianist George Winston recorded his first solo piano album in 1972, for John Fahey's Takoma Records. The album, *Ballads and Blues*, disappeared without much notice. But by 1980, when Winston recorded his *Autumn* album on Windham Hill Records, he had fully developed the melodic style of solo piano that he's known for today. Winston calls his style "folk piano" or, more precisely, "rural folk piano."

Windham Hill Records was founded in 1976 by Will Ackerman, a carpenter and guitarist who wanted to promote instrumental acoustic music. No one knows who coined the term "new age music," but that's what the music on the Windham Hill label began to be called. In 1981, Tower Records became the first record store chain to create a special section for new age music.

The term "new age" is somewhat unfortunate because it links the music to the spiritual and philosophical trend called the "new age movement." Several musicians who fall under the "new age" label have disavowed the term, preferring to call their music "contemporary solo piano."

However, *Billboard* regularly publishes a New Age Albums chart, the Grammy Awards hands out a trophy for Best New Age Album, and Amazon.com has a product category called New Age Piano. The fact is, the designation "new age music" has stuck to this day: we still refer to the solo piano music played by Winston, Jim Brickman, David Lanz, and others as "new age piano."

New age piano is most often performed by a soloist. George Winston, David Lanz, Kevin Kern, Scott D. Davis, Jon Schmidt, Liz Story, and David Nevue, to mention a handful of pianists, usually perform on solo piano. Yanni, John Tesh, Lorie Line, Ludovico Einaudi, Yiruma, and others generally perform with ensembles.

The Origin of the New Age Sound

New age piano is a synthesis of genres, including classical, jazz, and pop. One ancestor is the classical music of Erik Satie and Claude Debussy. (It should be noted that many new age pianists, such as George Winston, have never studied classical music.) Satie (1866–1925) was an eccentric French composer who referred to his works as "furniture music," by which he meant that it was intended to be background or ambient.

Satie wrote music that was deceptively simple and startlingly beautiful, such as his "Gymnopedie No. 1," an exquisite and graceful waltz that used modal harmony and major seventh chords long before they became fashionable in American jazz.

In "Gymnopedie No. 1," a bass note in the left hand precedes a sustained chord. The melody is played in single notes by the right hand. I've included chord symbols in the following excerpt.

TRACK 1

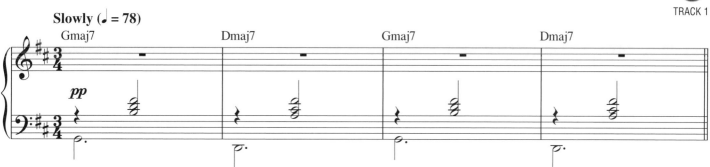

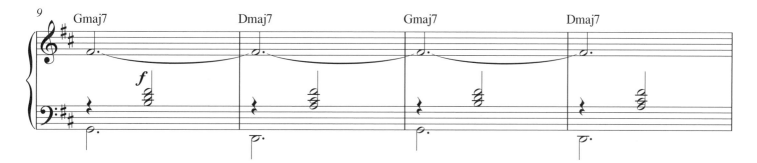

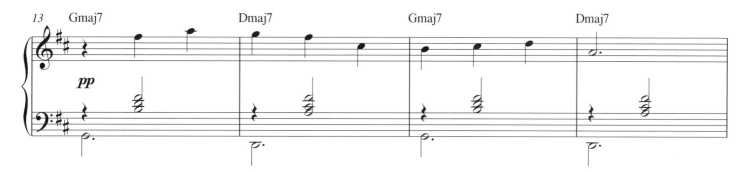

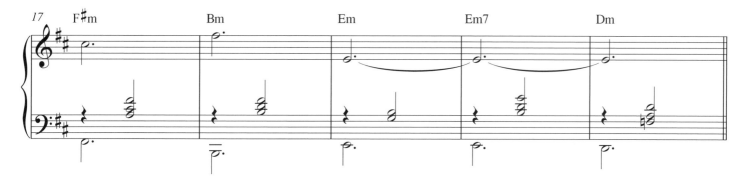

Other French composers called the Impressionists had a bearing on new age piano. Claude Debussy (1862–1918) gave evocative titles to his pieces – "Moonlight," "Clouds," and "Footsteps in the Snow." Typically, new age pieces also have evocative titles, such as "Leaves on the Seine," "February Sea," or "Wedding Rain."

Debussy's piano piece "Rêverie" is an example of the nascent new age piano style. It's serene and dream-like, with a lovely melody and beautiful harmonies.

TRACK 2

Expressively ($\downarrow$ = 100)

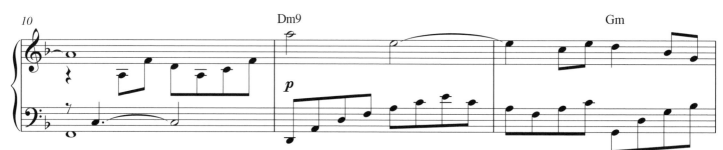

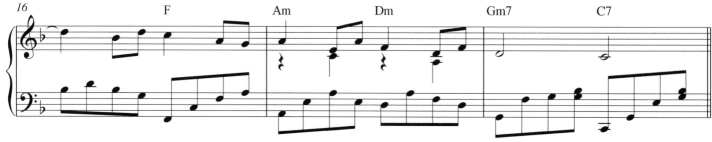

The great American jazz pianist Bill Evans (1929–1980) also had an effect on new age pianists, especially Liz Story. Evans's composition "Peace Piece" could be considered an early precursor of new age piano music, with its simple ostinato and improvised melody. The following example is in the style of "Peace Piece."

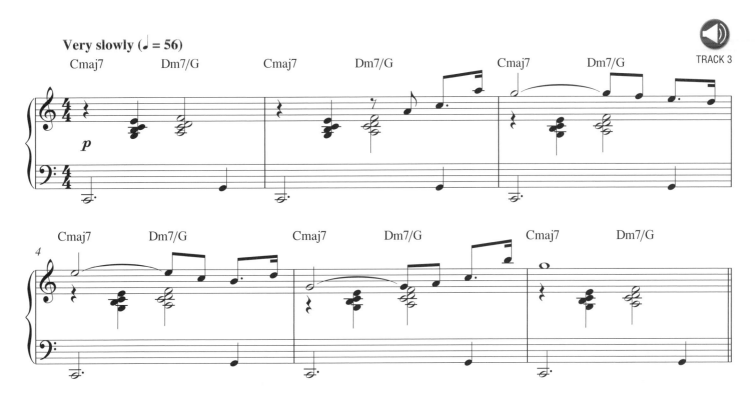

The American jazz pianist Vince Guaraldi (1928–1976), best known for his jazzy soundtracks for the *Peanuts* television specials, is another influence on new age piano music. George Winston has recorded two albums of Guaraldi's music.

Further influences on new age music include John Fahey, Leo Kottke, Brian Eno, Mike Oldfield, the Paul Winter Consort, and Oregon. The music of American minimalist composers Terry Riley, Philip Glass, and Steve Reich also guided new age music composers.

Keith Jarrett and the ECM Style

One of the greatest influences on the new age piano style was the improvised solo piano albums made by Keith Jarrett in the 1970s, especially his 1975 masterpiece *The Köln Concert*. This recording remains the best-selling solo piano recording of all time.

Jarrett (b. 1945) is an American pianist of awesome talent. *The Köln Concert* is a live recording of a concert Jarrett gave in Cologne, Germany. Jarrett's *modus operandi* at the time was to walk onto the stage, briefly acknowledge the audience, sit down at the piano, and then play whatever he was moved to play at the moment.

Jarrett has a prodigious technique and is blessed with a musical imagination of enormous scope. *The Köln Concert* reaches rhapsodic flights of inspired creativity that are almost mystical in their intensity. The music is punctuated by vamp-based passages that help ground the music in a funky and earthy way.

The Köln Concert was issued by the German ECM record label, known for its simple CD covers, with lots of white space and striking photographs. Jarrett's solo piano albums, along with the production and packaging of ECM records, became the blueprint for the whole genre of new age piano.

The Rise of Windham Hill

Windham Hill Records began in 1976 and followed ECM's lead in musical production and cover graphics. While ECM was geared toward contemporary jazz, Windham Hill leaned toward modern folk and blues. However, an early Windham Hill advertisement went so far as to call the label "an American ECM."

In 1980, the company released George Winston's *Autumn*, which became a huge hit. Windham Hill became the most successful new age label and the solo piano became the new age instrument of choice.

Other independent labels entered the picture, such as Narada in 1983. A host of new age piano players came along, including David Lanz, Michael Jones, Liz Story, Wayne Gratz, Philip Aaberg, Spencer Brewer, Suzanne Ciani, and Jim Chappell. Most of these pianists are still active.

Today's new age pianists are typified by the large group of players featured on the website www.solopianoradio.com, also known as "Whisperings." As of this writing, nearly 250 solo piano artists are represented by Whisperings. They generally eschew the new age label and more often refer to their music as contemporary solo piano. The Whisperings artists include the veterans Lanz, Chappell, Ciani, and Gratz, plus several others discussed in the book.

Chapter 2

GENERAL CHARACTERISTICS OF NEW AGE PIANO

Let's start by making some broad stylistic observations regarding new age piano music.

Meter

While the majority of today's pop, rock, and hip-hop music is written in 4/4 meter, new age music often uses triple meters, such as 3/4, 6/8, and 12/8 – in addition to 4/4. Yanni has written several compositions in 9/8, and he's composed music in such unusual meters as 7/8 and 10/8.

Tempo

Tempos of new age piano music lean toward the slow and moderate. By contrast, fast tempos are also played.

Rhythm

Rhythmic emphasis in new age is generally on a smooth and steady flow. Both eighth-note and 16th-note rhythmic subdivisions are used.

Eighth notes are usually played as straight-eighths and not as swing-eighths as they are in jazz. There are rare exceptions, such as the swing-eighth notes in George Winston's "Rag," but in general new age music does not swing.

Rhythmic phrasing is usually fairly "square." Two and four bar phrases, within eight- or 16-bar sections is the norm.

Dynamics and Expression

New age music is generally played at softer volumes than rock or jazz. However, some new age piano music can be quite powerful and loud.

Most new age music is played *legato* (i.e., smoothly). Nevertheless, this is just a general observation. George Winston's piano style features a sharp attack that gives the piano a ringing, bell-like quality.

Chapter 3
HARMONY

On his official website, George Winston recommends learning music theory, which he says is essential to his own musical approach. The best place to start, he says, is with learning chords. We'll take Winston's advice and begin with a review of chord theory.

Chord Types

A chord is a collection of three or more notes played simultaneously. Our Western harmonic system is based on **triads** – three-note chords built by stacking major and minor thirds.

Four triad types can be built by stacking major and minor 3rds – major triads, minor triads, diminished triads, and augmented triads. New age piano uses major and minor triads frequently, but uses diminished and augmented triads sparingly. Here are the four triad types, built on the root C.

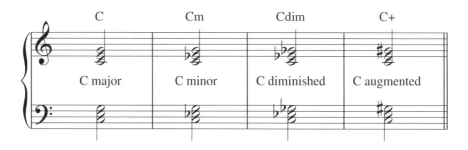

If we build triads on each degree of the C major scale, we create diatonic triads. Following are the diatonic triads for the C major scale.

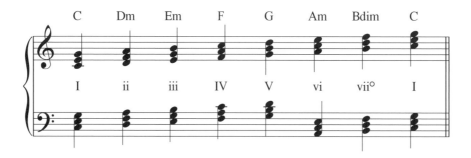

We designate a chord built on a specific degree of the scale with Roman numerals. Upper-case Roman numerals indicate major chords and lower-case Roman numerals indicate minor or diminished chords. We also name chords by the letter name of the chord root in upper-case letters followed by the chord type in lowercase letters. A capital letter by itself indicates a major chord.

A 7th chord is a four-part chord in which another 3rd is added to a triad. The common 7th chords used in new age piano are the major 7th, the minor 7th, and the dominant 7th.

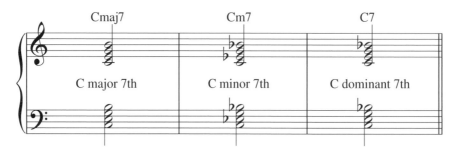

Here are the diatonic seventh chords for the C major scale.

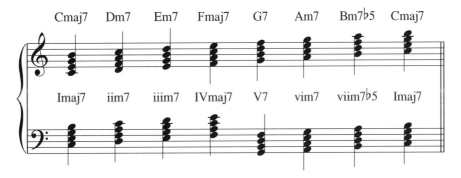

Ninth chords are five-part chords in which another 3rd is added to a 7th chord. The 9th chords used in new age piano are the major 9th, the minor 9th, and the dominant 9th.

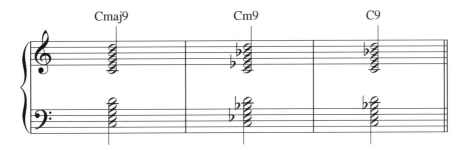

Both major and minor 6th chords, which are triads with an added 6th, are used in new age piano.

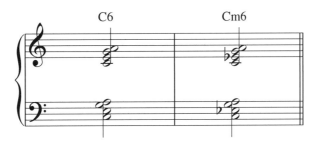

Both major and minor add2 and add 9 chords are used in new age piano. An add2 chord is formed by adding to the triad the interval of a 2nd above the root. The same holds true for the add9 chord. It's the same pitch, but is voiced an octave plus a 2nd above the root. The slight dissonance of the second lends a special quality to the add2 chord.

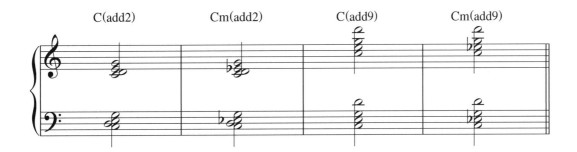

There are many other chord types, but these are the ones that predominate in new age piano music.

Chord Inversions

New age piano makes liberal use of chord inversions. An **inversion** is a chord with a note other than its root on the bottom. "Root position" has the root on the bottom. "First inversion" has the 3rd on the bottom. "Second inversion" has the 5th on the bottom. Here are the inversions for a C major chord and a C minor chord.

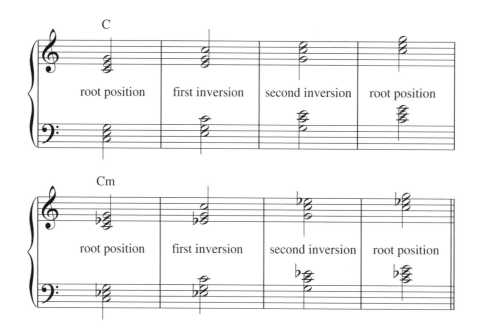

Four- and five-part chords can be inverted, too. Here are the inversions of both Cmaj7 and Cm7 chords.

Slash Chords

Sometimes a chord symbol will be two different letters separated by a slash. A **slash chord** indicates a chord in which the bass note (i.e., the lowest note) is not the root of the chord. The letter before the slash is the chord name and the letter after the slash is the desired bass note. Thus, the symbol C/E means a C major chord with an E in the bass.

Chord Voicings

It's important that you know the notes in chords. However, you not likely to voice chords on the keyboard in simple ascending stacks of 3rds. A keyboard **voicing** is a specific allocation of notes between the hands, chosen to interpret the chord symbol in question. The chord tones may be spread out, doubled, or missing altogether. The chords may be played by one hand or both hands. Chord symbols do not indicate voicing. Voicing is up to the performer.

When the notes of a chord are placed closely together, the chord is said to be in **close position**. When the notes are spread out more widely, the chord is said to be in **open position**.

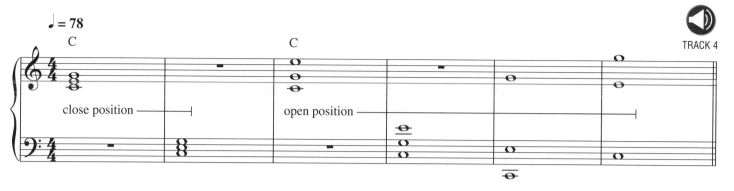

Track 5a is a **close** voicing for Dm7. Track 5b is an **open** voicing for Dm7, created by moving the 3rd and 7th of the chord to a different octave. 5c is a more open voicing for Dm7. In Track 5d we've doubled the D in the left hand and the A in the right hand. 5e is a close voicing in first inversion and 5f is an open voicing in second inversion.

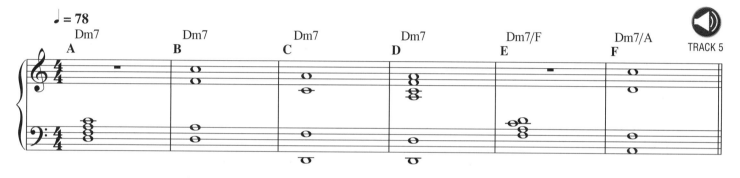

Sometimes, an interesting chord voicing can be used as the impetus for an entire new age piano piece. For instance, George Winston begins "Rain" with open-spaced major 7th chords in first inversion. Winston plays the chords entirely with his left hand. The next example is in the style of "Rain."

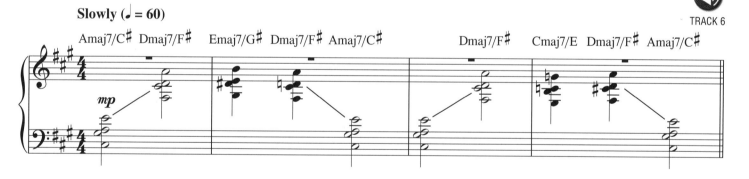

Peter Buffet used a voicing of an add2 chord in first inversion prominently in his song "Northern Morning." The next example replicates that style.

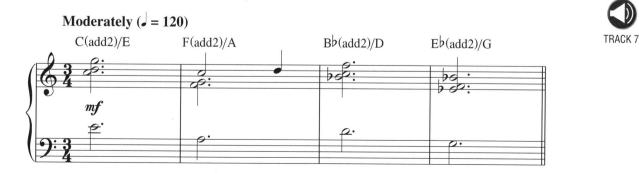

In Winston's "Longing," there's a part where he plays open-voiced chords similar to the following example. Please note that Winston can reach an interval of a 10th with either hand. If you cannot reach 10ths, you can simply roll the chords.

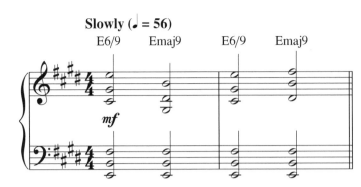

You should experiment with chord voicings and find ones that appeal to you.

Chord Progressions

A **chord progression** is a sequence of chords that progress logically from one to another. Jazz and pop musicians call the chord progression for a song the "chord changes" or simply the "changes." Musicians often work with a chord chart that tells them in shorthand fashion the changes for a song.

New age chord progressions tend to move fairly leisurely. There is no urgency to make a chord change. Sometimes a single chord will be used for several consecutive measures. Winston's "Cloudburst" uses a single chord for the entire song.

Traditional pop music is often based on the ii–V–I progression, where root movement of the chords is up a 4th (same as down a 5th). But new age piano music generally uses different kinds of root movement, such as falling or rising 2nds, falling or rising 3rds, and falling 4ths.

In the following example, Figure A illustrates falling 2nds as chord root movement and is in the style of David Nevue's "A Moment Lost." Figure B shows rising 2nds as root movement in the style of Nevue's "A Voice in the Wilderness." Figure C uses falling 3rds as root movement in the style of Kevin Kern's "The Enchanted Garden." Figure D illustrates rising 3rds as root movement, and Figure E uses falling 4ths as root movement.

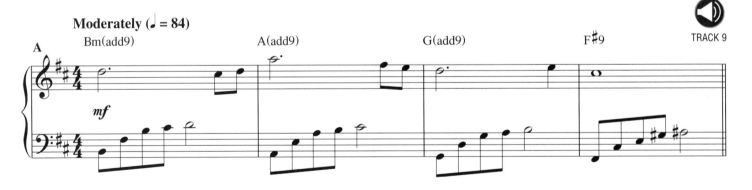

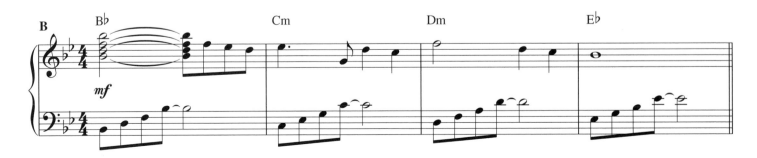

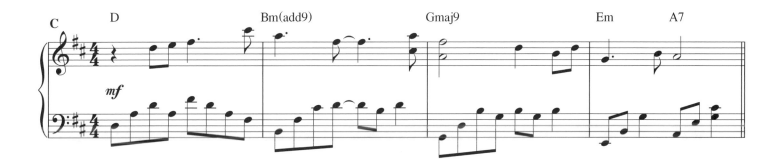

A common new age chord progression is simply the alternation of two chords, such as George Winston's alternation of A(add9) and Bm(add9) chords in "Colors." Winston plays broken chords with a passing 9th on beat 2 in each bar. Because he uses the sustain pedal to run the notes together, the 9th is essentially a part of each chord.

Slowly ($\quarternote$ = 76)

TRACK 10

The following example, in the style of Kevin Kern's "Children at Play," uses the same two chords as Bill Evans's "Peace Piece." (See Track 3.)

Moderately ($\quarternote$ = 92)

TRACK 11

Yiruma based his entire popular instrumental ballad "River Flows in You" on a two-bar, four-chord progression similar to the following example. The roots progress down a 3rd, down a 4th, and down a 4th.

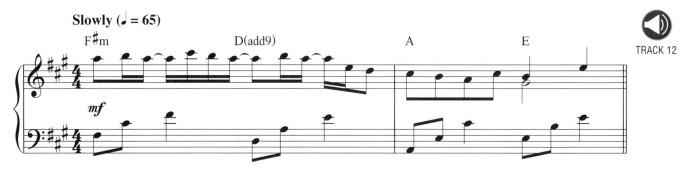

Jim Brickman's harmonic stock-in-trade seems to be chord progressions using primarily I, IV, V, and vi chords. The following example is in the style of his popular instrumental "Angel Eyes."

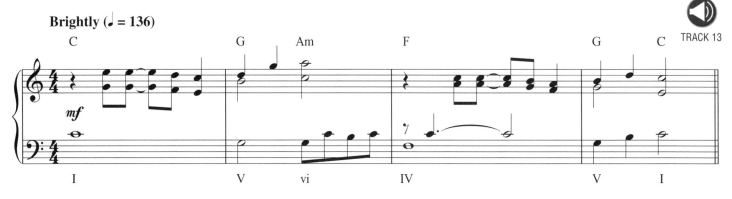

The next example is in the style of Brickman's "Winter Waltz," which also employs I, IV, V, and vi chords.

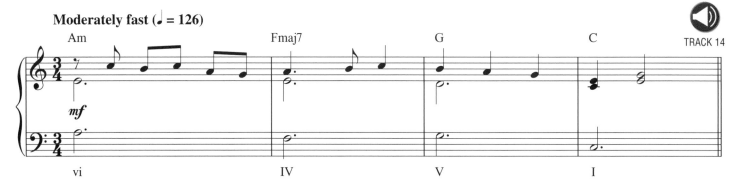

A common chord progression played by many new age pianists comes from Johann Pachelbel's "Canon in D Major" (The Pachelbel Canon), one of the most popular pieces from the Baroque era. George Winston recorded a version, as did David Lanz. Winston spells it "Kanon" and plays the piece in C. Jon Schmidt calls his version "Pachelbel Meets U2." Following is the main melody and four-bar chord progression of the Canon. The four bars are repeated many times with variations in both hands. The chord roots progress primarily down a 4th or up a 2nd.

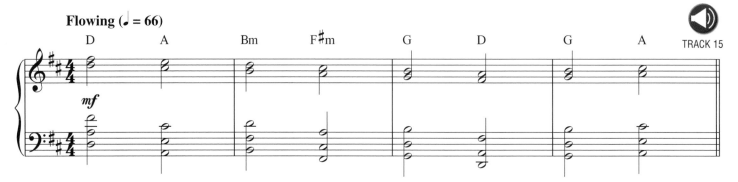

George Winston's "Thanksgiving" is built on a six-bar progression played first by the left hand alone. The progression is then repeated many times while the right hand plays in an improvisatory manner. The following example, written for left-hand only, is in the style of "Thanksgiving." Chord root movement is primarily down a 5th.

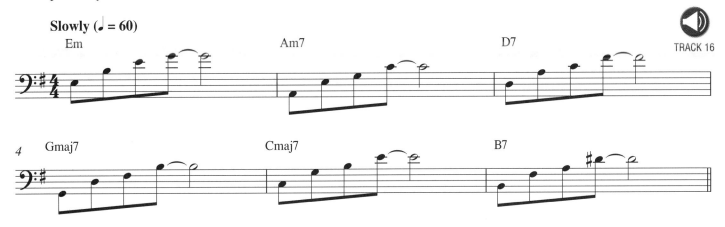

The next example is in the style of Winston's "Longing," which shows that you can make an interesting passage using just three chords and root movement by 2nds.

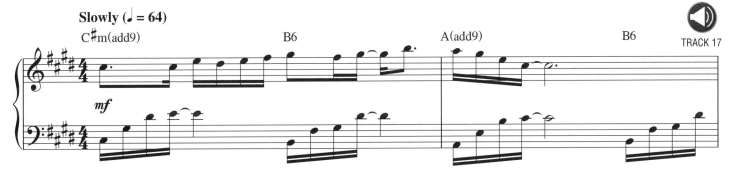

The Italian pianist/composer Ludovico Einaudi is a master of the two- or four-bar progression, which he then repeats many times with slight variations. Einaudi is a minimalist composer. **Minimalism** is named for its repetitive and pattern-oriented nature. The essence of minimalism is to draw out the process of musical change so that the listener becomes aware of the process. The next example is in the style of Einaudi's "Dietro Casa," with root movement down a 3rd, down a 4th, and down a 4th.

Track 19 is in the style of Einaudi's "Resta Con Me," with root movement up a 3rd, down a tritone, and up a 3rd.

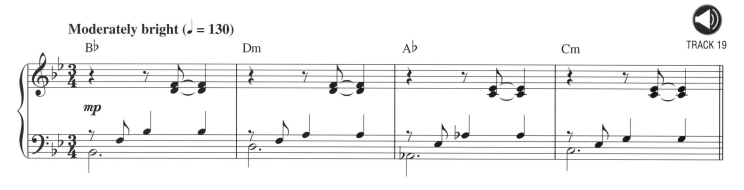

The following track is in the style of his "Bye Bye Mon Amour," which simply alternates two chords.

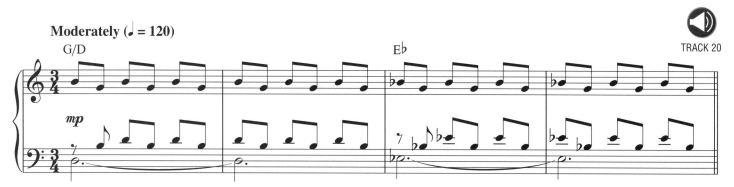

Chapter 4

LEFT-HAND ACCOMPANIMENT STYLES

Texture in music is its fabric. The simplest is **monophonic**, which means single-voiced. Thus, a melody without accompaniment is a monophonic texture. Occasionally, this is used in new age piano music. Winston's version of Alfred Burt's Christmas carol "Some Children See Him" both begins and ends with an unaccompanied statement of the melody.

Polyphony is another kind of musical texture, in which two or more melodic lines are combined in counterpoint, such as in J.S. Bach's *Two-Part Inventions*. Polyphonic writing is rarely used in new age piano music.

Homophony is used most of the time in new age piano music. Here, a melody is accompanied by chords. This usually means that the right hand plays the melody and the left hand plays chords in various accompaniment styles, which we'll now examine.

Arpeggios

The most common left-hand accompaniment style in new age piano is the arpeggio or broken-chord style. The notes of the chord are not played simultaneously, but in succession in a harp-like manner. Most often, these are eighth notes, but quarter notes and 16th notes are used as well. The beauty of the arpeggio style is that the left hand provides the bass note, the harmony, and a rhythmic background all at the same time. It is customary to use the sustain pedal to help emphasize the harmony. However, be aware that too much sustain pedal will make the music sound muddy.

Probably the most famous new age piano arpeggio pattern is the one that begins Winston's "Colors." The pattern is an alternation of two chords – A(add9) and Bm(add9). The chords are voiced as root/5th/10th, with a passing tone of a 9th in both chords. The pattern is played 11 times at the beginning of "Colors" before it changes.

TRACK 21

The next example features some possible variations of the "Colors" pattern.

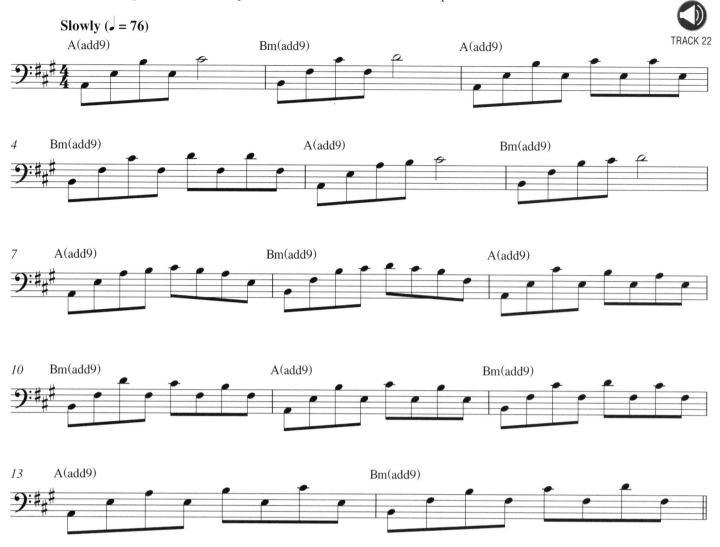

Later in "Colors," other interesting chord voicings are used in the arpeggio, similar to the following example.

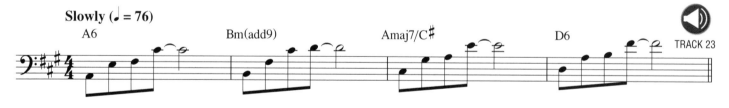

The next example is in the style of David Lanz's "Dream of the Forgotten Child." It also includes passing 9ths on each arpeggio.

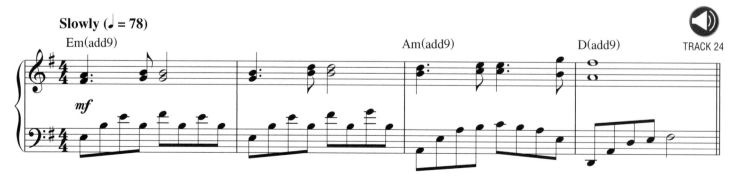

Arpeggios can be voiced in close or open position. The preceding examples are in open position. The next example is in close position in the style of Yanni's "To Take... To Hold."

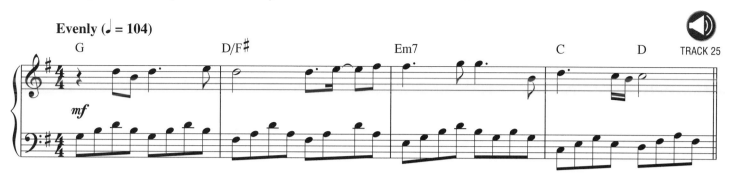

The next example features open-position arpeggios, covering a span of two octaves, in the style of Yanni's "Before I Go."

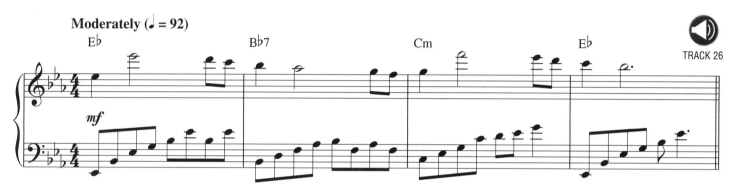

Most arpeggios last the length of a bar or less. Two-bar arpeggios, covering a span of more than two octaves like the following, are common in Suzanne Ciani's music.

Let's look at a few patterns in 3/4 time. The next example, in the style of Lanz's "Return to the Heart," uses root, 5th, and 10th, with the last two bars including a passing 9th.

The next example, in close position, is in the style of Brian Crain's "Rain."

Arpeggios are also commonly performed using 16th notes. Following are some examples. The first is in the style of David Lanz's "Madre de la Tierra."

Track 31 is in the style of Joe Bongiorno's "Always with You."

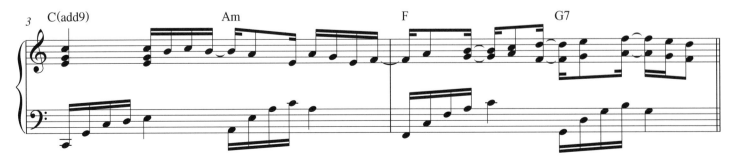

As with any piano style, "hands separate" practice is recommended for new age piano. In the arpeggio style, the left hand should keep a steady, even pulse. Practice simple arpeggios before attempting those that are more complex. When working on arpeggios, practice slowly at first and then work up to speed.

Block Chords

Another common form of new age piano arrangement consists of a melody played by the right hand accompanied by sustained block chords in the left. The block chords can be in open or close position. The beginning of "The Pachelbel Canon" contains an example of block chords in open position played by the left hand. If you cannot reach the interval of a 10th, simply roll the chords.

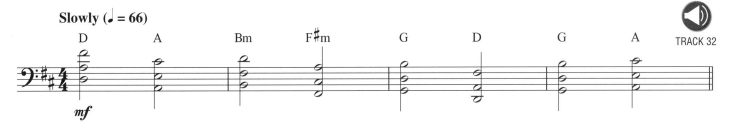

A gentle rhythm can be added to block chords in open position, as in the next example in the style of Lanz's "Summer's Child." Again, if you cannot reach an interval of a 10th, roll the chords.

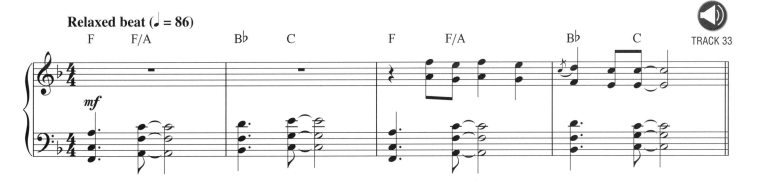

Block chords can also be used in close position, as in the next example in the style of Scott D. Davis's "A Simple Reflection."

Block chords can be played on each beat to create a regular, even pulse. The next example is in the style of Lanz's "The Setting of Two Suns." In measures 1–4 the chords are in close position, and in measures 5–8 the chords are in open position.

It's possible to put the repeated block chords in the right hand and the melody in the left hand, as in the first four measures of the example below. A related idea is to cross the hands and to play the melody in the bass register with the right hand, as in measures 5–8.

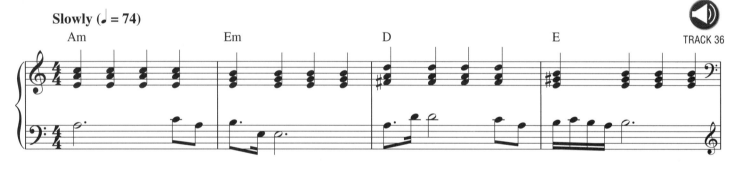

You could play the repeated block chords in an eighth-note rhythm, as in the next example.

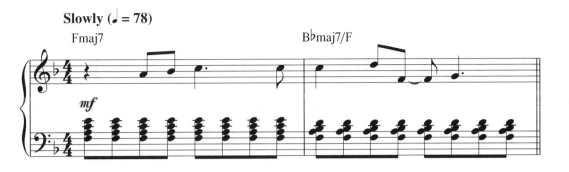

TRACK 37

Track 38 illustrates that both major 7th chords and add2 chords work nicely as repeated chords.

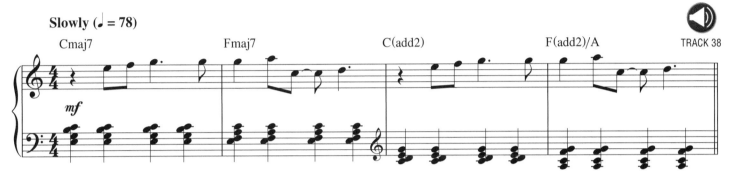

TRACK 38

Rolling Four-Note Patterns

Another type of left-hand accompaniment is what I call the "rolling four-note pattern." This is a group of four notes in close position played in an eighth-note or 16th-note rhythm. The four notes encompass a triad with an added 2nd or other interval as a passing tone. Often, by changing just one note in the pattern, you can achieve a welcome change of chord sonority. The next example is in the style of Yanni's "One Man's Dream."

TRACK 39

The next example is in the style of Lanz's "Dream of the Forgotten Child."

TRACK 40

Track 41 is in the style of Kevin Kern's "Remembering the Light."

"Cast Your Fate to the Wind" Pattern

A common left-hand pattern in new age piano comes from Vince Guaraldi's famous recording of "Cast Your Fate to the Wind." It's a one-bar rhythmic pattern in the left hand using the interval of a 5th. The pattern is repeated over and over.

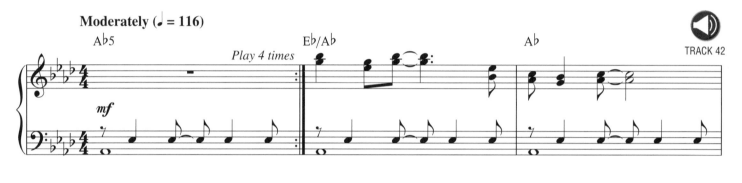

Track 43 is in the style of Jim Brickman, who used the pattern in "The Promise."

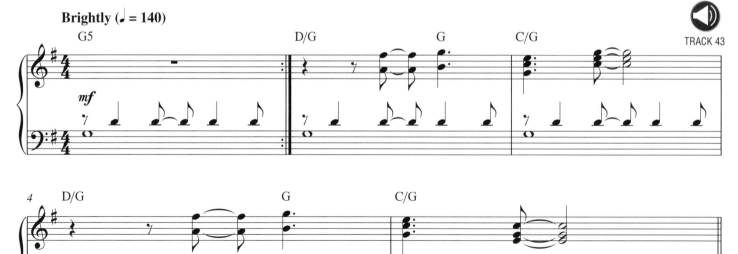

George Winston used a modified version of it in 6/8 time in "Stars."

Gymnopedie Style

The texture of Satie's "Gymnopedie No. 1" (Track 1) can be used effectively as a model for new age piano. It works well in 3/4 time. The components are the following: a bass note played on beat 1 followed by a sustained chord on beat 2, with a melody in single notes played by the right hand.

Stride Style

In stride piano style, the left hand plays bass notes on beats 1 and 3 and chords in the middle register of the piano on beats 2 and 4. Stride patterns are occasionally used in new age piano. Winston used stride patterns in "Road" and in his version of William Bolcom's "Graceful Ghost." The next example is in the style of Winston's "New Hope Blues."

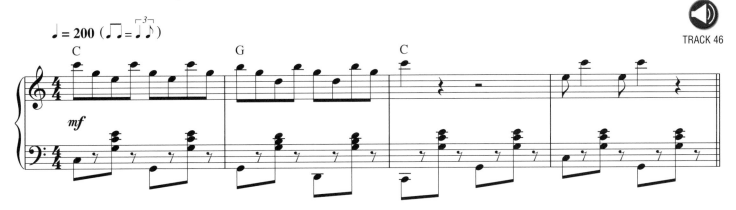

Repeated Notes

Simply repeating one note as a series of eighth notes can be an effective accompaniment pattern. The next example is in the style of Liz Story's "Solid Colors."

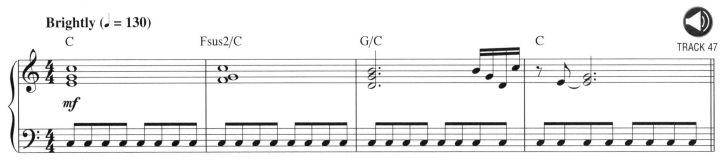

3+3+2 Patterns

David Lanz and Wayne Gratz both use a left-hand pattern in which broken chords in eighth notes are grouped into a rhythmic pattern of 3+3+2. The simplest version consists simply of the root, 5th, and octave of the chord, as in the next example. It is in the style of Lanz's "Behind the Waterfall."

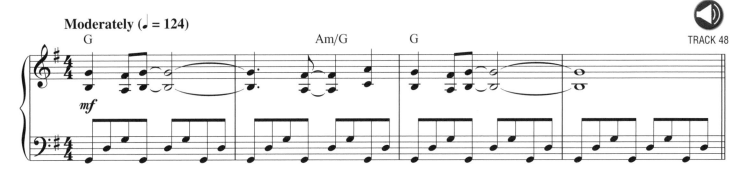

Lanz also uses the pattern with major 7th chords (without the 3rd). In the next example, in the style of his "Dream Field," the right-hand melody follows the rhythm of the left hand.

Triplet Patterns

Eighth-note triplet patterns work well in the left hand. In the next example, in the style of Lanz's "Vesuvius," a two-beat pattern of eighth-note triplets is played by the left hand. The pattern outlines an Am7 chord, with no 3rd.

TRACK 50

Track 51 illustrates left-hand triplets in close position in measures 1–4, while measures 5–8 illustrate triplets in open position.

TRACK 51

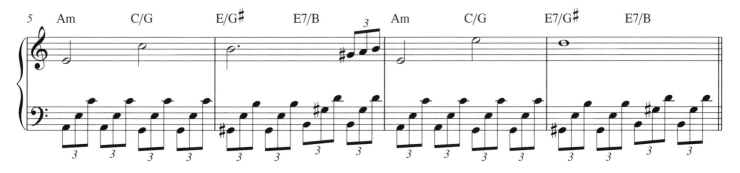

Melody in the Left Hand

At times, the melody can be found in the left hand while the right hand plays accompaniment figures. The next track is in the style of Jim Chappell's "Lullabye," in which the right hand plays an accompaniment figure in constant 16th notes, while the left hand plays the melody.

Ostinatos

An **ostinato** is a musical phrase that repeats persistently. Ostinatos most often occur in the left hand as accompaniment figures.

In George Winston's "Woods" there's a long improvisatory section over a one-bar left-hand ostinato built from two chords: E and E/A. The right hand plays freely in E Lydian mode. Track 53 is in the style of "Woods."

Track 54 is in the style of Wayne Gratz's "Green Room," in which an ostinato is built from the tonic and dominant notes of the key of A major, repeated as quarter notes.

The next track is in the style of Lanz's "Spiral Dance," which features a left hand ostinato outlining an E♭maj7 chord, but omitting the 3rd – which gives the chord a fresh sound.

An ostinato doesn't have to be in the left hand. Here's an example of an ostinato in the right hand, outlining an Fsus2 chord, with the melody in the left hand.

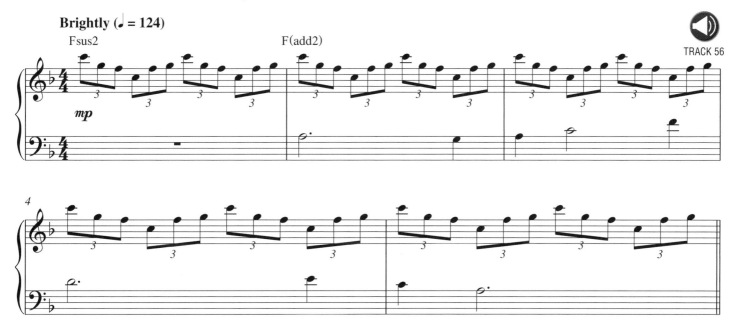

With all ostinatos, practice the pattern alone until you can play it smoothly and fluidly without thinking about it. This will allow you to improvise with your right hand without worrying about your left hand.

Chapter 5

MELODY

What Is a Melody?

In an instrumental piece, the **melody** is the musical line that you can hum or whistle. In most new age piano pieces, the melody is the top line played by the right hand. A melody has two basic components: a series of pitches and a rhythm. A good melody is memorable, recognizable, and has an emotional mood. Also, people enjoy hearing it again and again.

The Major Scale and the Minor Scales

Melodies in new age piano are generally tonal (i.e., in a specific key) and diatonic (notes adhere to the key signature, with few accidentals). They are most often based on either the major or minor scales. The major scale is also known as the Ionian mode and the natural minor scale is also known as the Aeolian mode.

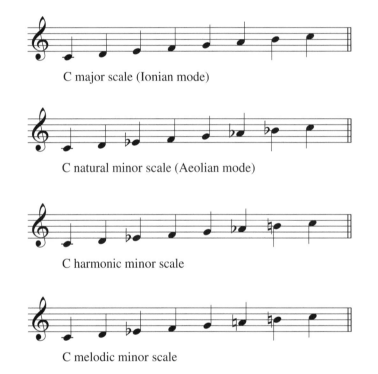

C major scale (Ionian mode)

C natural minor scale (Aeolian mode)

C harmonic minor scale

C melodic minor scale

The Modes

A **mode** is a division of the octave into half steps and whole steps. Each mode has a distinct musical personality because its half steps and whole steps fall in different places. Occasionally, new age piano uses one of the modes.

The **Dorian mode** consists of the white notes on the piano from D to D. It is like a natural minor scale with a raised 6th.

D Dorian mode   C Dorian mode

The **Phrygian mode** consists of the white notes on the piano from E to E. It is like the natural minor scale with a flatted 2nd.

E Phrygian mode   C Phrygian mode

The **Lydian mode** consists of the white notes on the piano from F to F. It is like a major scale with a sharped 4th.

F Lydian mode   C Lydian mode

The **Mixolydian mode** consists of the white notes on the piano from G to G. It is like a major scale with a flatted 7th.

G Mixolydian mode   C Mixolydian mode

The **Locrian mode** consists of the white notes on the piano from B to B. It is like a natural minor scale with both a flatted 2nd and a flatted 5th.

B Locrian mode   C Locrian mode

Pentatonic Scales

Pentatonic scales are also used in new age piano. The major and minor pentatonic scales each have only five scale tones. The major pentatonic scale includes the 1st, 2nd, 3rd, 5th, and 6th degrees of the major scale. It can be found on the piano by playing the five consecutive black keys starting on G♭. The minor pentatonic scale is based on the 1st, 3rd, 4th, 5th, and 7th degrees of the natural minor scale.

C major pentatonic scale   G♭ major pentatonic scale   C minor pentatonic scale

Melodic Motion

Melodies in new age piano are – generally speaking – broad, sweeping, and romantic.

A melody can move from note to note in three possible ways:

- **Stepwise motion:** moves up or down to a neighboring note by an interval of a half step or a whole step

- **Leaping motion:** moves up or down by an interval of a 3rd or a larger interval

- **Static motion:** stays on the same note

New age melodies utilize all three possible motions. Stepwise motion lends a smooth, flowing quality to a melody. And remember that you don't always have to follow a melody note with a different note. You can use static motion. Most new age piano melodies also employ leaping motion. Leaping motion in one direction can be balanced out by stepwise motion in the opposite direction. Likewise, stepwise motion in one direction can be balanced out by a leap in the opposite direction.

The next track, in the style of Yanni's "Reflections of Passion," demonstrates all three types of melodic motion. There are two leaps upward in the first three bars. But bars 4–8 are primarily stepwise motion, with a few instances of static motion.

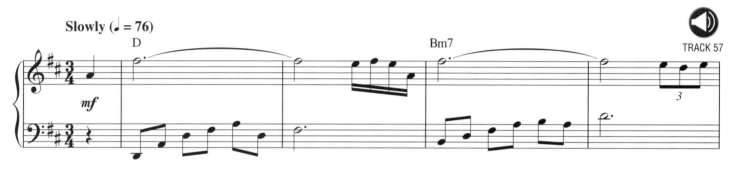

The following example, in the style of Yanni's "Nostalgia," features a leap in bar three that is emphasized by two grace notes.

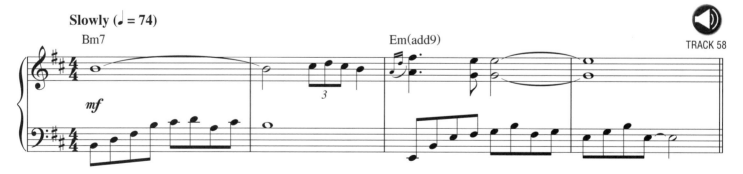

Track 59, in the style of Yanni's "Before I Go," contains two large leaps upward that are each balanced out by stepwise motion going down.

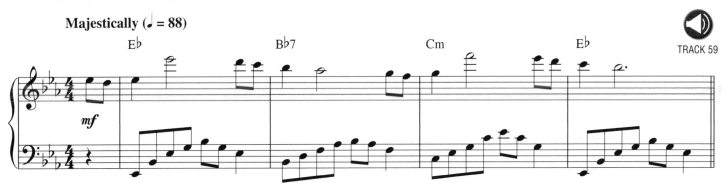

The figure below is in the style of David Lanz's "Leaves on the Seine." It features two leaps upward in bars 1 and 3, balanced out by stepwise motion moving down in bars 5–8.

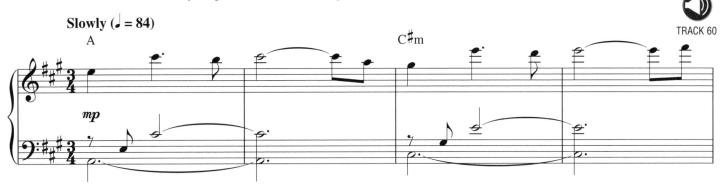

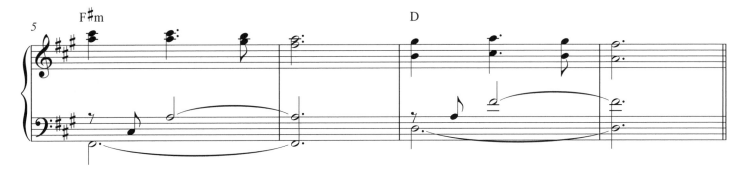

The next example is modeled after Lanz's "Before the Last Leaf Falls" and is based on a different premise – falling intervals of a 6th, evoking the falling leaves.

The following example, in the style of Jim Brickman's "Freedom," demonstrates how he incorporates syncopation into the melody when he plays in a moderate or slow tempo.

Many new age pianists intersperse a repeated 16th note (usually the tonic or dominant note of the key) between the melody notes of a phrase. Track 63 contains two examples. The first in in the style of Winston's "Woods," and the second is in the style of Nevue's "Overcome."

The final example here, in the style of Yanni's "Enchantment," demonstrates his propensity to write in unusual time signatures. This piece is in 9/8 time. Yanni has also written compositions in 7/8 and 10/8 meters. Note that the melodic motion is entirely stepwise.

The Motive and Motivic Development

New age melodies are generally motivic. A **motive** is a small group of tones used as a unit in forming a melody. Probably the most famous motive in music history is the dramatic four-note motive that launches Beethoven's Symphony No. 5.

A motive is developed by repetition and contrast. Twelve different techniques have long been the mainstay of motivic development in melody writing. We'll illustrate these techniques using a motive similar to the one from George Winston's "Colors."

- The **motive** is stated in Figure A.

- **Literal repetition** is shown in Figure B. Sometimes the literal repetition will be an octave higher or lower.

- **Sequence** is demonstrated in Figure C. This occurs when a motive is repeated at a higher or lower pitch level. A rising sequence adds intensity to a melody.

- **Interval change:** one or more intervals in the motive is modified. Figure D

- **Fragmentation:** breaking the motive apart and repeating one of the fragments. Figure E

- **Extension:** lengthening the motive by the addition of new material. Figure F

- **Inversion:** turning the motive upside down. Figure G

- **Rhythm change:** altering the rhythmic values. Figure H

- **Ornamentation:** repeating the motive in an embellished form. Figure I

- **Augmentation:** slowing down the time values. Figure J

- **Diminution:** speeding up the time values. Figure K

- **Thinning:** the deletion of certain notes of the motive to strip it down to its essentials. Figure L

- **Retrograde motion:** playing the motive in reverse (changing the pitches only). Figure M

- **Retrograde inversion:** Turning the motive upside down and then playing it in reverse. Conventionally, one turns the motive upside down first and then it's taken in reverse. Figure N

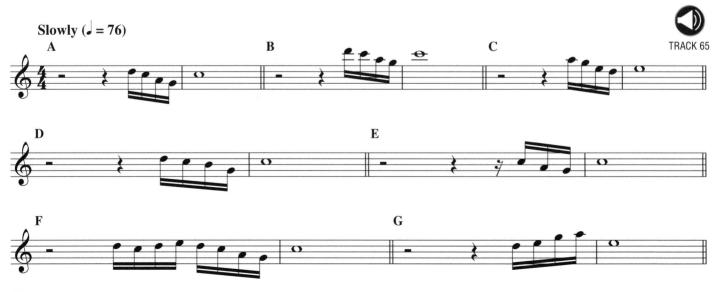

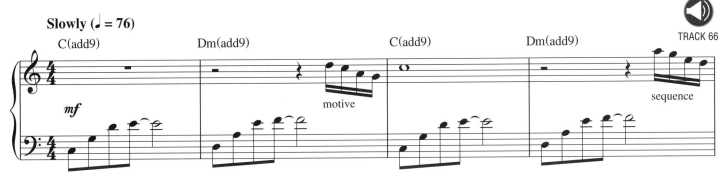

The following is a short piece that illustrates motivic development techniques in a practical context. It is based on our motive from Track 65.

TRACK 66

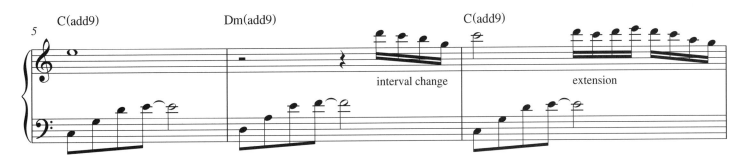

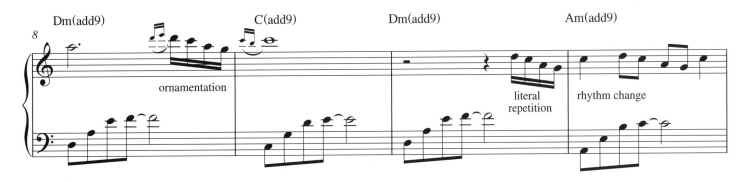

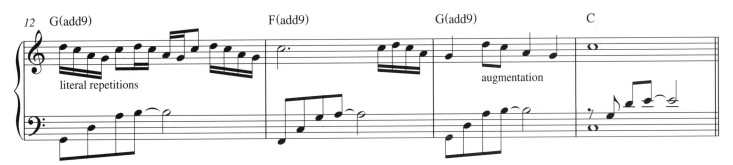

Chapter 6

DEVICES TO EMBELLISH A MELODY

New age piano melodies are often played as unsupported single notes in the right hand. However, melodies can also be embellished in several ways.

The simplest way to embellish a melody is to play it in octaves, as in the following track in the style of Lanz's "Courage of the Wind."

Another way to embellish the melody is to add 3rds under the melody line. In places where 3rds don't sound right, try 6ths instead. The next track is also in the style of "Courage of the Wind."

A third way to embellish a melody is with grace notes. A **grace note** is a short note that precedes the main note. The grace note usually "slides" by either whole step or half step into the main note, although intervals other than a half step or whole step can be used. In new age music, grace notes are usually applied from **below** the melody note. George Winston is an expert at grace notes. The following example, in the style of his "Reflection," shows how grace notes can make a melody more interesting.

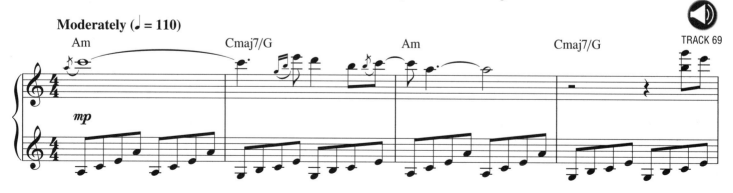

A series of grace notes can even form a chord, as in the following example. Play the grace notes on the beat, not before the beat.

Moderately ($\bullet$ = 110)

TRACK 70

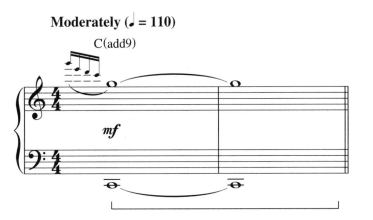

Chapter 7

SPECIAL EFFECTS ON THE PIANO

Hammering

Hammering is the technique of rapidly attacking one key with two fingers – it's like tremolo on one note. When Winston uses this technique, he uses his thumb and middle finger. He features hammering on the melody in "Moon" and near the end of his "Variations on the Kanon by Pachelbel." The next figure is in the Pachelbel style.

Sustain Pedal

Most new age pianists use the sustain pedal liberally. Winston often strikes notes very sharply with the pedal down and lets the notes ring out. The next track is in the style of his "Longing." Press the sustain pedal down and let the notes ring.

TRACK 71

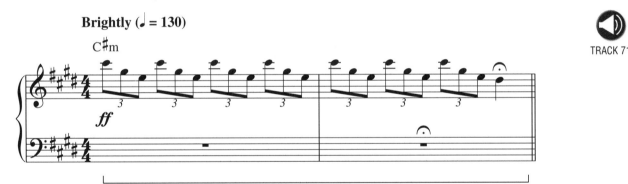

Tremolo

A **tremolo** is a rapid oscillation between two or more tones. In his "Sunrise," Michael Jones uses a technique similar to a tremolo. At the beginning of the piece he quickly and loosely repeats a pattern of six notes over and over with his left hand. When combined with the sustain pedal this creates a kind of background wash over which the melody is played. The next example is in that style.

TRACK 72

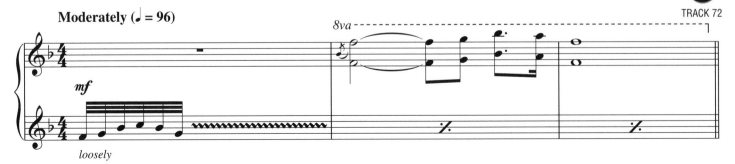

Chapter 8
SONG FORM

Form is the organizational plan of a musical composition. A work's form consists of the sections that make up the piece. Nearly always, predictable patterns recur in the songs you listen to and play.

The basic principles of song form are **repetition** and **contrast**. Basic song form consists of repeated sections varied with differing sections. We give the individual sections letter names (A, B, C, and so on) and indicate repeats of sections by showing the same letter.

Popular songs generally follow common patterns, such as AABA or ABAC. Form in new age music is less predictable. For instance, Winston's "Moon" is in the following form: AABBCCADEDEDEA. However, most new age pieces follow simpler forms and many are in standard song forms.

Most pieces begin with an **Introduction**, usually four to eight bars long. The **A Section** (the first main section), is generally eight to 16 bars long and usually features the main theme. The A Section then often repeats, with slight variations – such as the melody being played in a different octave or elaborated upon.

The **B Section** contrasts and does something different than the A section. Sometimes it's in a different key. The melody, harmonies, and rhythm usually differ in character from the A Section.

Sometimes there's a **C Section**. Many new age piano pieces also have a section in which the pianist can improvise over an ostinato or a repeated chord pattern. In most cases, the A Section returns in a restatement before the end.

The Coda is the ending bit. It often consists of a repetition of the last phrase.

The question of form should be looked at as an organizational unfolding, not as a preconceived mold into which the music is poured. Next time you are listening to new age music (or any popular music), try to identify the various sections.

Chapter 9
PUTTING IT ALL TOGETHER

We have examined techniques for building chords, voicing chords, putting chords in progressions, and using chords in left-hand accompaniment patterns. We have discussed melodic motion, motives and development, and building song forms. Now it's time to put it all together to make your own new age piano music

Q. Where do I start?
A. There is no right or wrong place to start.

You can start with a chord progression and try improvising a melody over it. Or you can start by noodling around on the piano until you've discovered a melodic motive and then develop the motive into a tune. One way to find a motive is to think in terms of a particular scale or mode. If you find a melodic idea, try to find some chords that support it.

You can even start with a particular left-hand accompaniment pattern. Choose a pattern. Find some chords that fit it and try improvising a melody over the pattern. Most new age pianists play their original compositions in basically the same manner from concert to concert. However, the compositions themselves were the result of many hours spent improvising and experimenting at the piano. One can assume that the pianists tried out various ideas and then began to separate the wheat from the chaff. Eventually, they developed and polished their musical ideas into fully developed, finished compositions.

Remember, you are not going to compose a finished piece of music in a few minutes' time or even in an extended session. Start by simply exploring the piano and its possibilities. If you find something you like, keep going. If you don't find something you like, try a different approach.

The great thing about exploring the piano in this manner is that it often yields unexpected results. Sometimes you simply stumble across something exciting – some chords that sound great together or a melodic phrase that really catches your ear.

When you find something you like, make sure you save it! If you are adept at music notation, write it down. If not, record it. Use a digital recorder or even your cell phone. If you have a keyboard with a sequencer, store it there. Lots of great ideas vanish when you rely only on your memory. Save your ideas and come back to them later.

Composing a piece of music is a bit like assembling a jigsaw puzzle. You have to consider your melody, harmonies, accompaniment styles, meter, tempo, dynamics, and form. You may have an idea in mind of what the finished composition should be like, but you have to fit all the pieces together.

Chapter 10
PRACTICE TIPS

Remember that we call performing on the piano "playing the piano." Play indicates that it's supposed to be fun. Fun is something done for its own sake and for the sheer joy of it.

The only way to improve on the piano is to practice. This requires time, effort, and discipline. However, practice doesn't have to be drudgery. Following are suggestions for enjoyable and productive practice.

1. Regular daily practice is better than playing for several hours once or twice a week. Choose times when you can relax and not be stressed out, distracted, or interrupted. Practice in a physically pleasant surrounding. The quality of practice is more important than the time spent.

2. Practice should be conscious, not mechanical.

3. Practice with a plan and goal in mind. What is it that you are trying to accomplish? Are you trying to learn a new song? Are you trying to tighten up a song you've been working on? Build on what you've already done.

4. Establish a comfortable fingering for each piece.

5. Often, when learning a new song, there seems to be too much happening at once. The best way to cope with a song's complexities is to disassemble the piece. Work on each song in sections and with each hand separately.

6. Isolate the song's various parts. Some parts of the music are likely to be more difficult than other parts. Work on the harder parts more than the easier parts.

7. Slow it down. Be patient. Hard parts become easier when played slowly. Also, slow it down to cultivate evenness and smoothness in your playing. Gradually work up to the proper speed. The goals of practice are smooth and even playing, playing at the correct speed, and playing expressively.

8. Try recording your practice to evaluate whether your playing sounds like you think it does. You may hear things (good and bad) that you're not aware of. Keep your recordings and date them. If you ever feel like you're not progressing, go back and listen to an earlier session to see how much your playing has improved.

9. Improve your rhythmic sense by playing with a metronome.

10. Take every opportunity to play with other musicians and singers. Music is meant to be shared.

11. Listen to piano recordings and attend live performances.

12. Never let yourself say, "I can't do it." Instead, say, "I haven't done it... yet!"

Chapter 11
STYLE FILE

Here's where you get a chance to put into practice all the techniques we've covered. This chapter includes six tunes composed in different new age styles. These will allow you to see how various new age piano techniques work in context. The songs are presented roughly in order of difficulty, beginning with the easiest piece and with the hardest piece appearing last.

On the CD, the left-hand part is on the left channel and the right-hand part is on the right channel, so you can practice each hand's part separately by turning down one channel or the other. The last two pieces are recorded twice – once slowly and once at full speed.

1. Autumn Passing

The first piece is in the style of George Winston's "Colors." It's in 4/4 time at a moderately slow pace. The key is G major, with the one departure from the key being the Fmaj9 chord at bars 36–38.

Harmonically, the piece is built around the alternation of two chords – G(add9) and Am(add9), presented in the left hand in eighth-note arpeggios with a passing 9th on beat two of each chord.

After a four-bar intro, the eight-bar A Section begins with a melody based on a four-note motive. This motive is developed using standard motivic development techniques. At bar 13, the A section repeats with a countermelody added to the right hand.

An eight-bar B Section begins at bar 21. Colorful voicings of the chords Gmaj7/B and C6 are used in the left hand. The C Section begins at bar 29. This section features block chords in the left hand and, at bar 32, two-handed voicings of mostly major 7th and minor 7th chords. After a pause on the Fmaj9 chord, the A section returns and is played twice. The piece ends with a short Coda.

TRACK 73

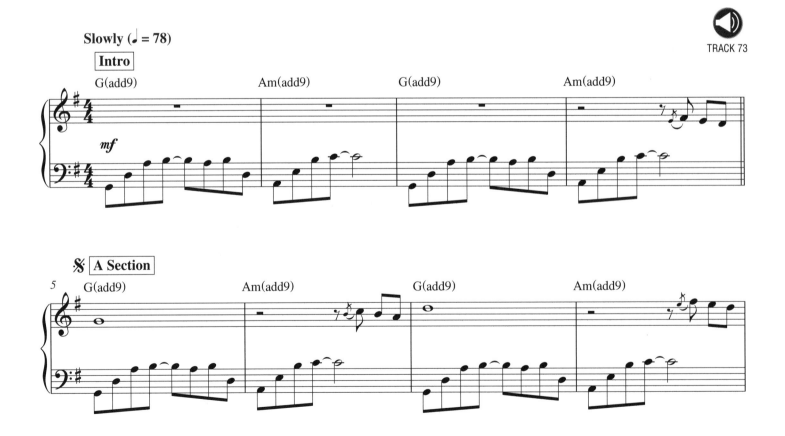

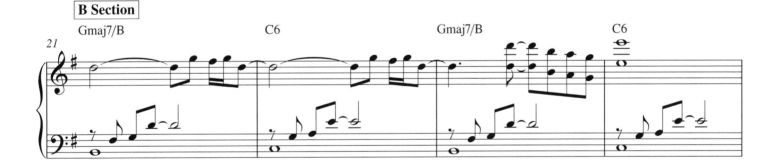

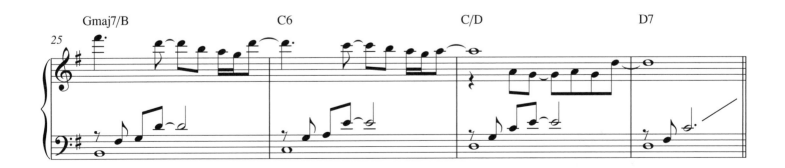

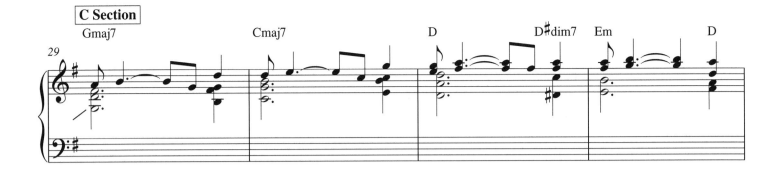

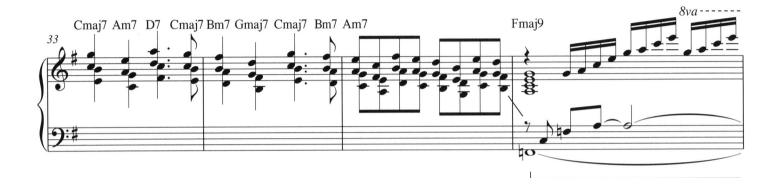

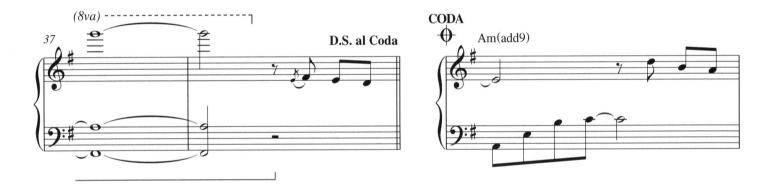

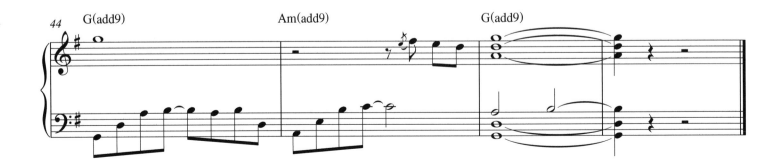

2. Cascades

This tune is in 4/4 time in a bright tempo in the key of Eb major. It's based on a 3+3+2 pattern of eighth notes in the left hand similar to patterns used by Wayne Gratz and David Lanz. The right-hand melody in the A Section is embellished by the addition of 6ths.

At the B Section, starting at bar 17, the right hand turns into a 3+3+2 pattern of eighth notes outlining an Ebmaj7(no 3rd) chord.

The C Section, beginning at bar 27, uses a left-hand pattern of eight eighth notes outlining an Ebmaj7(no 3rd) chord, while the right hand plays a syncopated melody using mainly the Eb major pentatonic scale. The song then returns to the first theme and ends with a short Coda.

TRACK 74

Brightly (♩ = 120)

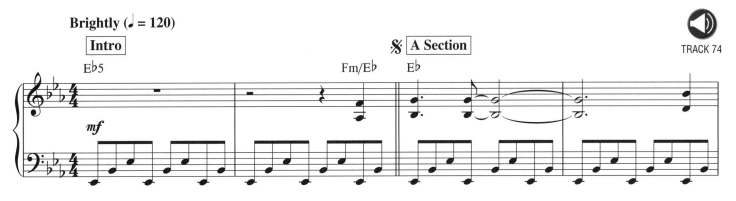

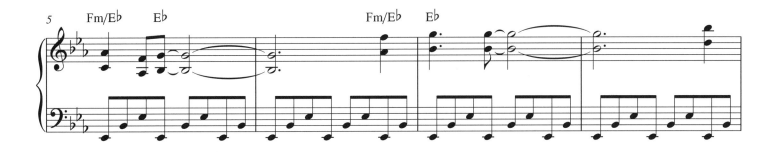

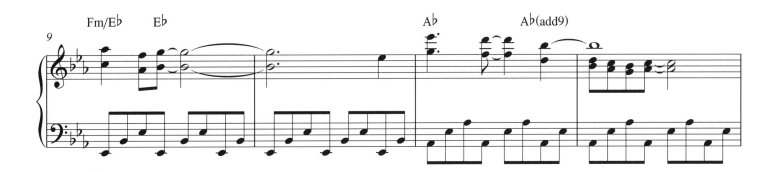

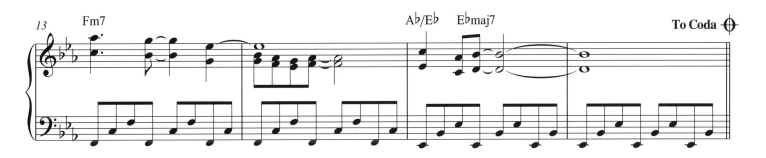

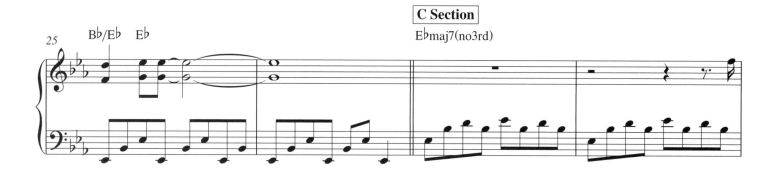

3. A Maple Leaf in the Pond

This tune is a graceful waltz that has stylistic elements similar to those of Jim Brickman, Kevin Kern, David Nevue, Jon Schmidt, Lorie Line, and David Lanz. The tempo is slow and the key is D major. Occasionally, the melody and harmony depart from the D major scale, such as in bars 7–8 and bars 21–22.

Melodically, the piece is built upon the variation of a two-bar, four-note motive. Harmonically, the piece is based upon a descending bass line: D-C♯-B-B♭-A-G♯-G.

The A Section (bars 1–16) has the left hand using simple three-note broken triads in open position in the treble register of the piano. The melody in the right hand is played in the very high register of the piano.

The B Section (starting at bar 17) uses 3rds in the right hand to embellish the melody, while the left hand employs broken chords in the bass register in a stream of eighth notes.

In the C Section, starting at bar 25, the right hand plays three-note patterns against the six-note patterns in the left. The A section then returns with the melody, sometimes embellished with 6ths. A simple Coda ends the piece.

Slowly (♩ = 72)

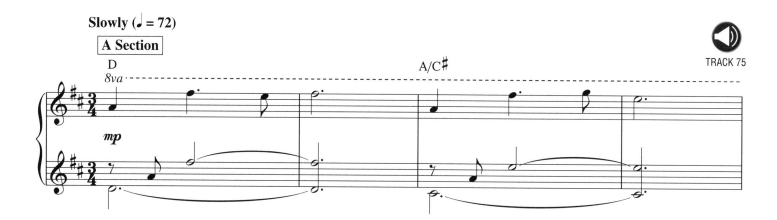

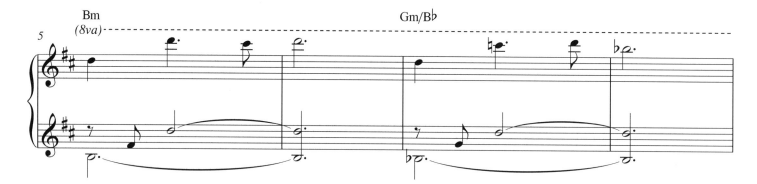

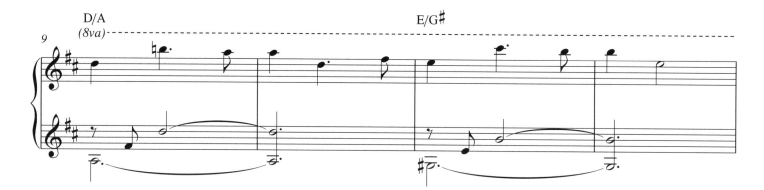

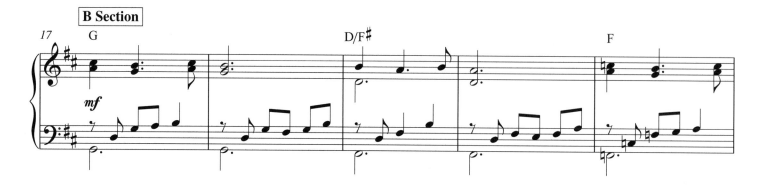

52

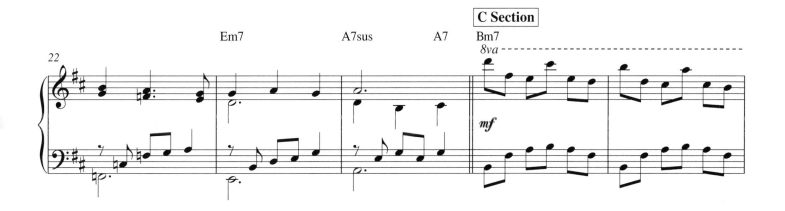

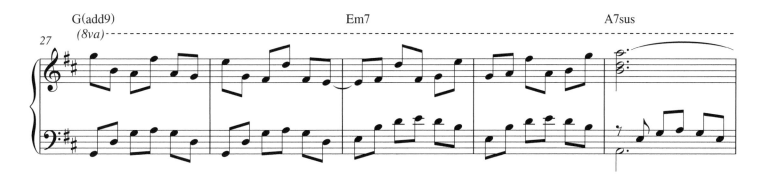

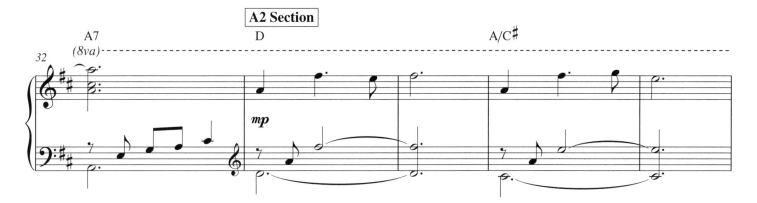

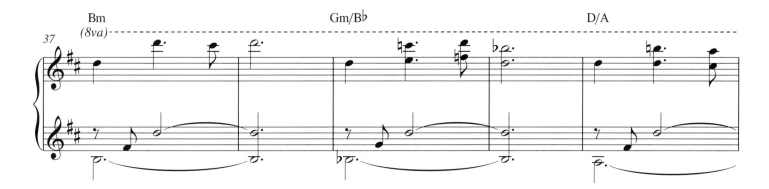

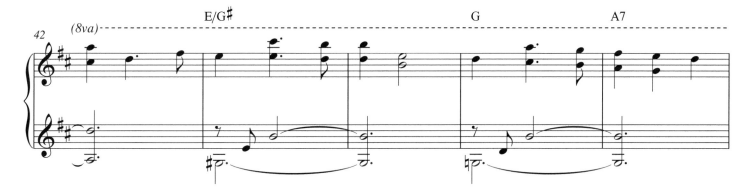

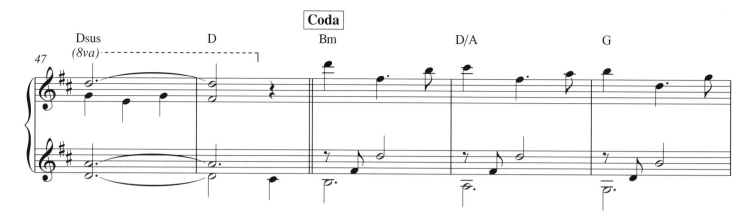

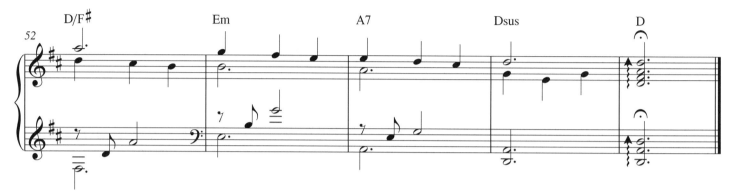

4. The Way of Passion

This piece is in moderately slow 9/8 time in the key of C major and is written in the style of Yanni, with much romantic gusto.

It begins with a short Intro featuring four-note block chords in close position played by the left hand in the treble register of the piano. Over this, triplet figures in the high register of the piano are played by the right hand.

The main theme begins at bar 7. The left hand switches to arpeggio patterns in open position at bar 11 and continues in that manner until the Coda. The chord progression beginning at bar 15 uses a lot of minor 9th chords. Both the melody and the chord progression tend to wander, moving through various keys and never quite settling on one. The root movement of the chord progression is primarily down a 5th. The right-hand melody is thickened with either octaves or four-part chords.

The B Section, beginning at bar 24, is quite similar to the A Section. It also wanders about melodically and harmonically.

The piece ends as it began, with a Coda featuring right-hand triplets in the high register of the piano over four-note, close-position block chords in the left hand.

TRACK 76

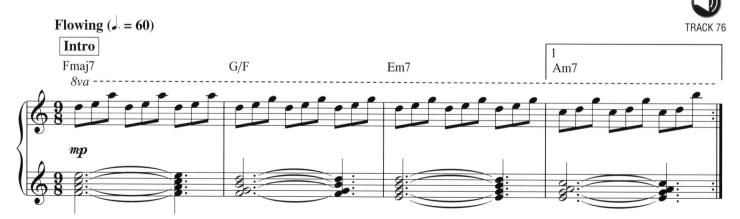

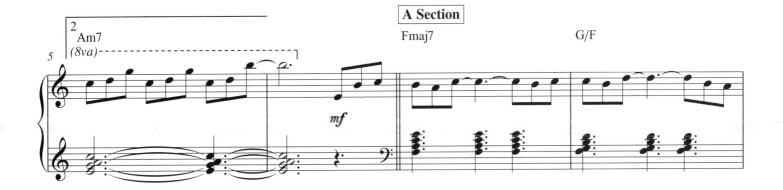

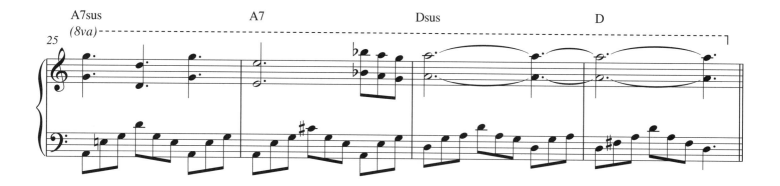

B Section

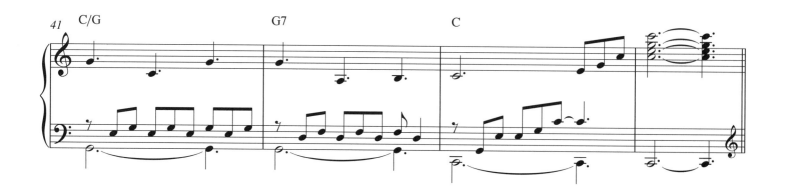

Coda

Fmaj7   G/F

5. Stargazer

This piece features extensive use, both harmonically and melodically, of the E♭ minor pentatonic scale (i.e., the black notes on the piano keyboard; see page 33). The piece demonstrates that playing on the black keys can be a very gratifying experience. The first 16 bars are played entirely on the black keys. The first white key (C flat) is played at bar 17.

The piece is in 4/4 time, played at a moderate tempo. It's in the style of David Lanz's "Reverie" and also has stylistic elements similar to Stephan Moccio.

The piece begins with a one-bar ostinato played by the left hand – a series of eighth notes outlining an E♭m7 chord, with an added A♭ passing tone. The pattern should be played smoothly and with an even flow. The sustain pedal can be used liberally.

In the Intro (bars 1–10), the right hand plays intervals of either a 5th or 6th in the high register. A melody begins at bar 11, embellished by the addition of either 3rds or 4ths. Starting at bar 19, the melody is essentially repeated with some different chords in the left hand.

At bar 27, the two hands play streams of eighth notes in contrary motion for two bars. Then the left hand keeps playing eighth notes, while the right hand plays eighth-note triplets for a bar and then 16th notes for a bar. This creates cross-rhythms with the left hand. This rhythmic technique is out of the minimalist playbook of Philip Glass.

At bar 35, the original left-hand ostinato returns while the right hand plays four-note block chords in the high register. The piece ends in G♭ major, the relative major key of E♭ minor.

TRACK 77
Slow Speed

TRACK 78
Full Speed

Moderately (♩ = 112)

Intro

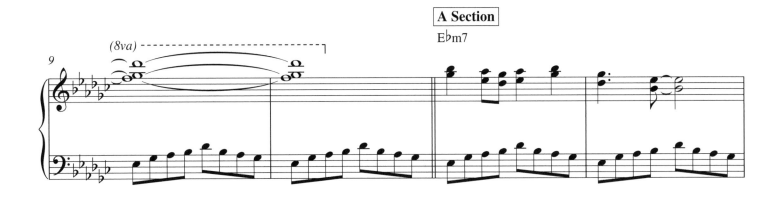

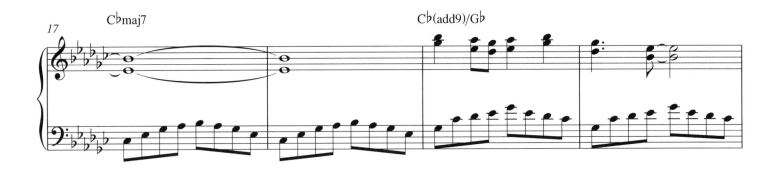

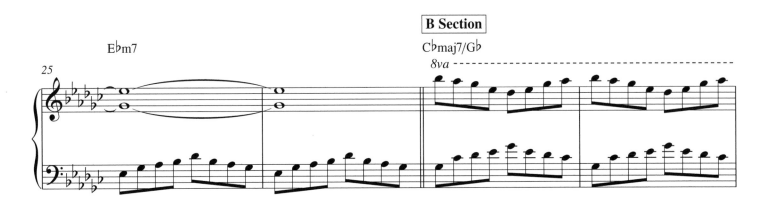

F♭maj7♭5

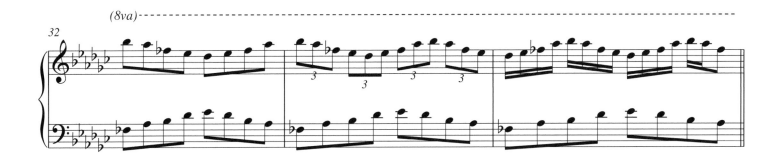

Coda

E♭m7

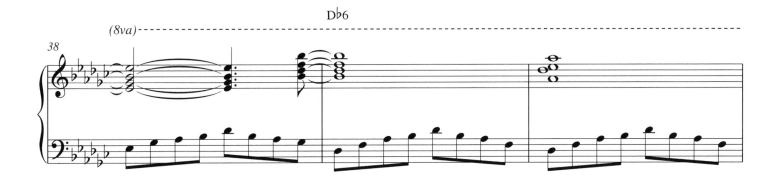

D♭6

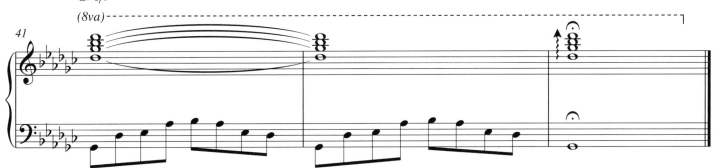

G♭6/9

6. Dance of the Planets

This tune is written in 4/4 time, played in a quick tempo, with a constant triplet feel on each beat. It has stylistic elements similar to Scott D. Davis, Stephan Moccio, and David Lanz.

The left hand begins with a two-beat ostinato in eighth-note triplets, outlining an Am7 chord (without the 3rd). The right-hand melody at the A Section (bar 4) uses lots of 6ths and some octaves. There are harmonic changes at bars 9 and 10, and then the left hand returns to the original ostinato.

The B Section begins at bar 21 with a triplet pattern in the right hand that repeats over Am7, Fmaj7, Dm7, and B♭maj7 chords. At bar 28, there's a C Section that uses a one-bar ostinato in the right hand with a melody in the left hand thickened by three-note, open-voiced triads, including many in inversions.

The piece returns to the beginning to reiterate both the Intro and the A Section, before it ends with a short Coda.

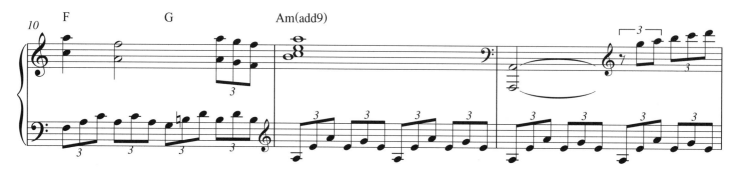

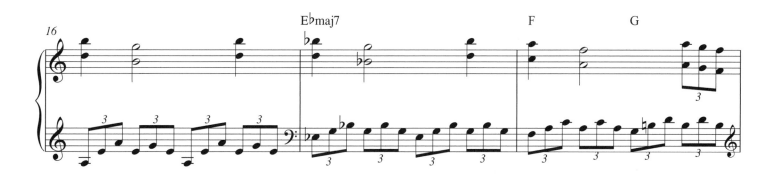

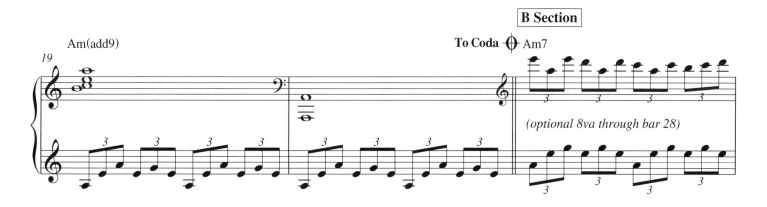

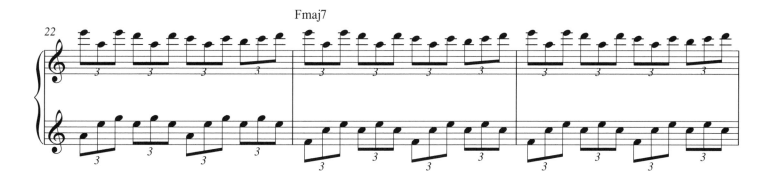

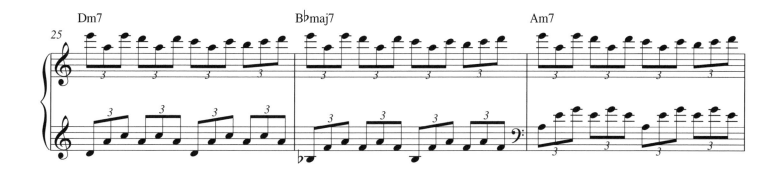

C Section

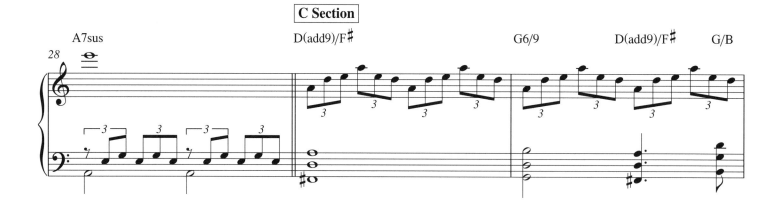

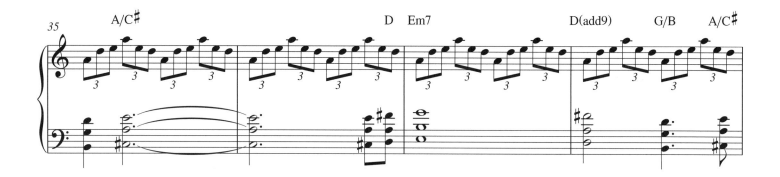

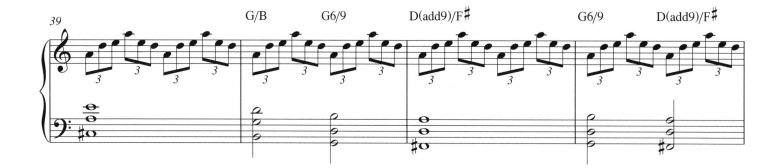

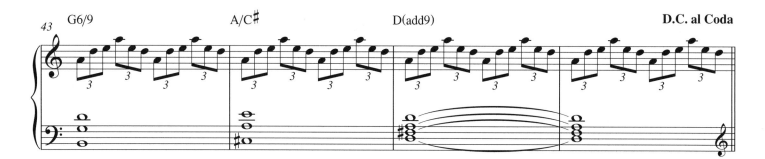

CODA

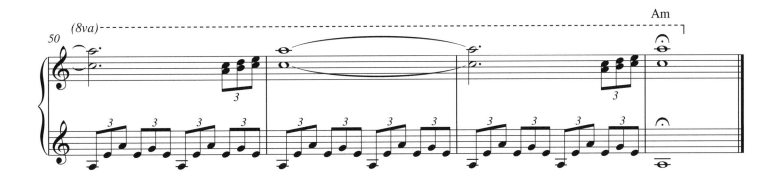

NEW AGE PIANISTS

A Short List

Philip Aaberg
Omar Akram
Joe Bongiorno
Spencer Brewer
Jim Brickman
Suzanne Ciani
Brian Crain
Scott D. Davis
Ludovico Einaudi
Wayne Gratz
Doug Hammer
Isadar
Tim Janis
Michael Jones
Bradley Joseph
Peter Kater
Brian Kelly
Kevin Kern
David Lanz
Lorie Line
Stephan Moccio
David Nevue
Jon Schmidt
Liz Story
John Tesh
Michael Whalen
George Winston
Yanni
Yiruma